TRIPLE YOUR TIME TODAY!

10 Proven Time Management Strategies To Create & Save More Time

Kathryn McKinnon

medical, accounting, or tax advice.

The purchaser or reader of this publication assumes responsibility for the use of these materials and information, including adherence to all applicable laws and regulations, federal, state, and local, governing professional licensing, business practices, advertising, and all other aspects of doing business in the United States or any other jurisdiction in the world. No guarantees of income are made. Publisher reserves the right to make changes. If you can't accept these terms, kindly return the product. The Author and Publisher assume no responsibility or liability whatsoever on the behalf of any purchaser or reader of this material.

http://www.Kathryn-McKinnon.com
http://www.Kathryn-McKinnon.com/blog
http://twitter.com/KathrynMcKinnon
http://www.linkedin.com/in/KathrynMcKinnon
http://www.facebook.com/pages/Kathryn
McKinnonCoaching

Introduction

Time is a serious issue these days. Whether you're in business for yourself or you work for someone else, executives, entrepreneurs and professionals have way too much to do and not enough time to do it. Your life is crazy. You want more time to do the things you'd like, but you're bogged down with too much work, too many responsibilities and not enough time to enjoy the life you've made for yourself.

With the information contained on these pages, you're in a better position to achieve your goal of maximizing and freeing up your time. You'll learn what you can do to quickly develop a set of strategies to find more time in your day to *Triple your Time* so you can enjoy your life.

Why should you listen to me?

Let me give you a personal example of this formula in action. I've been an executive for 32 years and an executive coach for the past 20 years helping executive women, entrepreneurs (and open minded men) learn how to achieve more success with their life, career, and their Time. I'm an entrepreneur and the founder of two businesses. I'm a busy mom with two active boys and a husband who travels extensively. Essentially, I'm a single mom when my husband is away for weeks at a time. I'm also a paid professional singer on weekends (*which I also love*), I create and market beautiful custom-made gemstone jewelry with meaning, www.DAIKOMYO.com and I volunteer for a number of local organizations.

I'm the one responsible for keeping things going smoothly with all our schedules, driving the kids to school, keeping track of after school sports and activities, managing my own schedule and my businesses. It's important to note, *I don't work 14 hour days*, I generally keep weekends open for family activities, I work from a home office and *I don't have a full time assistant.*

By the way, I also wrote and published this book in less than 90 days and it made the Best Seller list for its Category on Amazon in less than 6 weeks.

It's a lot to handle and I could become overwhelmed, but I'm able to do it all with relative ease. Now, I share all this at the risk of sounding like I'm bragging, but that's not my intention. I want you to see how I'm getting the important things done so I can enjoy my family and we can have a comfortable life together; I can enjoy my work and still have time to do the other things I'm passionate about.

How do I do it?

Over the years, I've developed a specific *mindset* as well as *systems* that essentially allow me to create more time for the things I need and want to accomplish. I've been the **assistant editor** of a regional magazine. I was a **production editor** managing and delivering over 300 multi-lingual projects within 12 months and on budget for the Marketing Division of the 1980 Lake Placid Olympic Organizing Committee. I've been a **product manager** for a major U.S. Commercial Bank and **directed** the Career Management and Executive Education Divisions at Harvard Business School, *managing relationships with thousands of Corporate Executives and Recruiters.*

Through trial and error and many mistakes, I've created a System to manage multiple

projects, lead teams, manage and coach executives, run a household, manage two businesses, raise a family and simultaneously manage my time, successfully and without a lot of stress. It took me years to figure out the system that was right for me…
…A system that allows me to achieve maximum results in my business and personal life, without compromising my nature as an effective entrepreneur, a compassionate human being, and a feminine woman, wife and mother.

I haven't always been so effective with my time.

My career in commercial banking is a good example. My bosses and mentors were men. And while I learned some very useful strategies for managing my time from them, they were, *men*, so I thought I had to act like them and mold myself to fit the roles they were modeling for me in order to be successful.

I put in the 14-hour days--I was the last one to leave the office. I had little personal life and was totally consumed by the job. I read all the popular business and time management books and enrolled in courses to keep up and try to get ahead. I was stressed out, overwhelmed, and my health began to suffer.

What happened next changed my life.

While driving home from an off-site conference, I was lost in thought about the events of the day and what I still had to accomplish…***I never saw the Truck***.

In a flash, a two-ton flatbed truck ran through a stop sign and violently broadsided my car. My car came to a stop in the middle of the busy intersection. The car was totally crushed except for a *tiny little space* behind the steering wheel where I'd been sitting. I was lucky…I lived.

I seriously think my angels saved my life that day. I only suffered minor bruises but had a concussion and severe back pain. After a brief visit to the hospital, I returned to work several days later. But after months of physical therapy and one year of visits to a chiropractor, my back pain persisted… and so did the stress at work.

Then my boss gave me a copy of a book to read

about meditation. I was raised to believe in God. I certainly believed in the power of prayer and had always been a spiritual person but I knew nothing about meditation and I didn't realize it was a tool I could use to relieve stress.

I began to look at TIME in a totally new way.

As I began to read about the philosophy behind the practice, *I started to appreciate TIME in a totally new way.* I realized that all my attempts to be productive and successful had almost succeeded in helping me lose my life. Not only that, I didn't feel as though I had a sense of purpose or passion about what I needed to be doing with my life.

All the time I'd spent devoted to my work life had left me disconnected from my intuition and my feminine nature. I'd lost track of the true meaning of my life, my time and its value.

A New Beginning

Since then, which was many years ago, I've had a continual awakening in how to stay within my grounded personal energy while consistently moving toward my goals and getting things done.

I reclaimed my personal power. I found my purpose and embraced how I spend my TIME in a whole new way...life opened up for me and around me, smoothly, and with grace and certainty and it continues each and every day!

These experiences have helped me develop the inner tools and strategies to stay organized and focused, grateful and engaged in my life. I've developed a frame of mind--a way of thinking, that helps me successfully keep things on track, free up my time and reach my goals without becoming overwhelmed or giving up the things I love to do.

I also coach others on how to manage their time effectively. I've incorporated many Time Management Case Studies of my clients' Success Stories throughout this book to give you real examples of how I use these strategies to help motivated executives, entrepreneurs and professionals become even more successful with their life, career *and their Time.*

You can learn and use these strategies to free

up your time without having to wait 32 years or make the same mistakes I made.

You now have in your possession a book that will take you through the steps you need to take control over your time so you'll have more of it to enjoy.

Every effort has been made to make this book complete and accurate. As of the writing of this book, all the information is based on my current strategies.

This is much of the same information my clients pay thousands of dollars to obtain. If you use and apply these strategies, you'll find them to be an invaluable resource for the rest of your life.

Please put quiet time aside to read this entire book, even if you only read a chapter at a time. There is so much powerful information contained within these pages that to try to absorb it with distractions just wouldn't serve you.

I advise you to read this book in a way that helps you use your time effectively. Make an effort to implement these strategies and tactics daily as you read each chapter. I also encourage you to take notes in this book as you go along and to record your thoughts and insights.

The client time management case studies described in this book are true, although I've changed clients' names to protect their privacy.

Thank you for taking some of your precious time to read this book. I hope you begin to use these Personal Time Management Tips, Tools, Activities and Strategies now and work them into your daily routines to create new, productive habits so that you can *Create and Save More Time!*

Much Success,
Kathryn McKinnon

Contents

Triple Your Time Today!

10 Proven Time Management Strategies to Create & Save More Time

Forward

Do you know what your lost time is costing you? What would you do if you had more time to enjoy the life you've created?

Your Life is crazy. You're busy and stressed most of the time yet you feel like you're "spinning your wheels" and not moving forward in your career or business.

You've gotten caught in the shift in the economy, so you react to your day instead of planning what you need to do and you spend your time responding to urgent distractions and countless interruptions.

You procrastinate on important projects because other priorities take up your time and you feel like you never accomplish anything.

You want more time to focus on your needs to exercise, eat right, get enough rest, but you spend so much energy on your daily tasks and routines serving the needs and demands of others, you just can't find enough time to do the things you want.

You know you should spend more time with your spouse or kids or those you love, and you feel guilty about it, but you have a long list of emails and unreturned phone calls so you spend time "finishing up" at work instead.

Does this sound familiar? Where does the time go? Why can't you find the time to get everything done and have more time for yourself?

If any of this resonates for you, then you're in the right place. The strategies and tactics in this book will help you create the time you're looking for, to do more of what you want and end each day with a sense of accomplishment and freedom.

Strategy #1
Develop the Right Mindset

Why Can't You Find the Time?

Finding time to do more of what you want seems to be increasingly difficult. You're bombarded with requests and demands for your time. There are constant interruptions and distractions that take time away from what you should be doing and what you want to do.

There are pressures from your job, your boss, your colleagues, your family, and even friends. And because everything happens much more quickly in this electronic age, *you just don't have enough time to get everything done.* It's as if everyone wants your time and everyone but you succeeds in getting what they want. Why is that? Why can't you find more time for yourself, to do the things you want?

External pressures, being overwhelmed, over-commitment, poor planning, mindless routines, bad habits, interruptions, unexpected events, things getting in the way — these things all play a part.

So what's really going on here?

We all know we have 24 hours in every day. That means we have 1,440 minutes in every day. Which also means we have 86,400 seconds in every 24-hour period.

How do you spend those 86,400 seconds each day?

Do you know *how* you spend your time?

Do you remember what you did last week? Yesterday? Do you remember how you spent the last hour?

Do you remember what you thought about while you were spending your time?

Were you focused on your goal and what you were doing, or was your mind somewhere else?

If you're not getting the results you want with your time, then maybe it's because you're not choosing to focus on the right things.

You can become far more efficient with your time when you become consciously aware of what you're thinking about each moment.

If you really look at how you spend those 1,440 minutes out of each day, can you honestly say you're as efficient with your time as you could be? Do you really spend a full 8-10 hours of each and every day at home or at your job focusing and concentrating on reaching your goals? Are you really present in each moment? Probably not. It's pretty difficult for most of us to continually focus non-stop on a goal or task.

What about the constant distractions and interruptions? What do you do to avoid those speed bumps and roadblocks to your daily accomplishments? Do you stay focused? Or do you allow yourself to get distracted?

Time Management Case Study: Judy

Sometimes it seems impossible to focus on accomplishing goals when worry and fear are the distractions that consume all of your time and attention. That's when you have to remember what you actually have control over.

Judy was one such client. She had by all standards a great life that everyone envies. She had a great husband and happy family. She lived in a wonderful community with an excellent standard of living. She was intelligent and attractive and she had an excellent job but it was stressful. She had it all--*except her health.* She came to me as a woman recovering from breast cancer. She had recently undergone surgery. She was in a great deal of pain from the procedure and was experiencing numbness in her arms.

As we began to work together, Judy described her feelings of anger and her self-pity over why this had happened to her. She had researched all the statistics related to her particular type of cancer. But even though the doctors had caught it early, even though the surgery was successful and her prognosis was excellent, she didn't believe her doctors. She was convinced that the cancer would return.

Judy's mind was focused on her cancer and being sick, not on getting well.

Despite having it all, she had a very negative attitude about her life. She had grown up with this attitude about herself too. Despite the fact that Judy's doctors told her all the cancer had been removed, she admitted she was now focused on the *possibility* of developing cancer again. She was focused on the statistics showing that most patients have a recurrence of the disease.

Judy was living in fear that she still had cancer and was convinced she didn't deserve to be healthy. She was living in fear and worry about her health, about the world, the economy and situations around her that she felt helpless to control. *She had been thinking this way most of her life.*

Judy was worried about, and focusing on all the things in her life that were wrong and that she couldn't control.

If every moment of her time was spent on thinking about how sick she was, then how could Judy possibly focus on doing the things she needed to do to help herself get well?

Judy's own thoughts and negative focus were

creating even more stress in her life and this stress was affecting her health. She was faced with the ultimate challenge in her life--the prospect of running out of time to live.

She needed to change her focus and mindset before this *prospect* of dying became her reality. I told Judy what I tell all of my clients:

> ***You control very few things in life: You control your thoughts. You control your words. You control your feelings, and you control your responses.***

You simply can't be angry, worried or fearful <u>and</u> happy at the same time, so you have to choose which thought and emotion you want to live with each and every moment. Thoughts and emotions pave the way for how you respond and that leads to what you experience.

You are a powerful creator. With that power, you have freedom of choice and responsibility. Most of us create our experiences by accident. We don't create consciously, or with full awareness. I believe that's because we don't realize how very powerful we are. We just don't realize we can create our experiences. When you learn to focus your mind, you can become a powerful creator of wonderful experiences by choice rather than by chance. You can choose to create with full awareness rather than by chance or by accident.

You can choose at any given moment in time what you think, what you say, how you feel, how you respond and what you wish to create with your actions. You can create more of the worry and stress you experience by thinking more about what's bothering you, or you can choose not to allow stress to effect you in a way that hurts you or creates pain, discomfort or even disease. In every moment, you can choose to live your life focused on worry and fear or you can choose to make room for something more positive, something better. You can learn to Transform the negativity and even let it go!

First, however, you must understand you have the power to create your experiences and your life. A good thought creates the energy of a good experience. A fearful thought creates the energy and the experience of worry or stress.

- You choose your thoughts.
- Only you speak your words.
- You are the one who chooses what you do in any moment.
- You are the only one who lives your life.

You don't have control over anyone else, over their thoughts, their words or even their actions. Once you understand "what" you actually do control, then you can let the rest go and use that awareness to begin to create and transform the experiences in your life. When you do this, when you change the way you think on the inside, everything else around you changes on the outside.

When you are fearful or worried or under stress, always reach for a better thought. A good thought will create a better feeling and that will help you make better choices which will lead you to better responses, actions and experiences.

During several meetings together, Judy learned how to focus on the more positive aspects of her life and even began to see the cancer as a blessing. She began to see it a gift given to her to help her transform her attitude and her life. I taught her new strategies to help her use her time to shift her focus, to create positive intentions and to focus on one day at a time while setting positive goals for her future.

Her pain and numbness dissolved and she regained full function. She quit her stressful job and decided to focus on living a life of great health and gratitude. She developed a much more positive outlook about her life and now believes she deserves to be happy and healthy. She currently works in a less stressful job and remains cancer-free.

You may not believe you have control over your time because of the demands others make of you.

However, you do have control over how *you think* about any situation. You have control over what you think about when you spend your time. You have control over the priorities you choose to act upon. You have control over how you respond to a situation before you take the time to do anything.

When you create this kind of mindset, and think of your time in this way, you begin to live with a greater sense of awareness and freedom about what you choose to do with the time you have.

If you take action right now and implement this one strategy into your daily routine by consciously choosing your thoughts, you will begin to DEVELOP THE RIGHT MINDSET to create and save more time!

Strategy #2
Do the Right Things
At the Right Times

How do you *spend* the time you have?

The human brain has an amazing ability to allow us to do one thing and simultaneously think about something totally different. This can happen when we multitask, when tasks become routine or when we let our mind wander. Have you ever been driving your car, only to reach your destination and not remember for an instant how you got there? Your subconscious mind took over for an instant and directed you there, even though your conscious mind was somewhere else.

Have you ever gone to retrieve something only to get there and forget what it was you were there to get? I certainly have. This happens when you're not focused on what you're doing, when you're *unconsciously present*.

You slip into autopilot as you work on tasks. Before you know it, you've lost your place and lost track of time. In this case, the time you've spent has been wasted.

Your time is a precious commodity.
Once it's gone,
You can never get it back.

It takes practice, training and concentration to stay focused. And it takes wisdom to make good choices about how to spend your time. You may not be able to normally stay focused for extended periods unless you really love what you're doing; however, if you realize that within every minute of every day you make choices about what you do, then suddenly you become a lot more aware of how you spend your time.

If you're doing one thing but your mind is somewhere else, you're not doing the right things at the right times.

You have to develop the right mindset and focus to position yourself for success at everything you spend time on. You must know what you want to accomplish in order to do the right things at the right times.

1. What are your **goals**?

2. What are your **intentions** for reaching your goals?

3. Are your **values** aligned with your intentions?

4. What are your **priorities** to make the best use of your time?

The answers to these questions require a certain level of engagement and commitment from you.

What you do with your time either yields results or it doesn't. If you spend your time doing the wrong things, you won't achieve the results you want.

Learning how to get more done is worth nothing if you're not working on the right things at the right times to move your career, business or dreams forward. Otherwise you're just filling up your time and "spinning your wheels."

Time Management Case Study: Rachael

Have you ever wondered where your time went? Sure you have…we all have at some point. We sit around looking back at the time we've invested and wonder where it went. If we had planned, organized, worked hard, and set goals, we would be looking forward wondering how to move beyond our already achieved goals.

But we didn't have a plan, we didn't set our goals straight, stay organized, or work to achieve the goals we planned. So we look back with regret about what we didn't achieve or accomplish.

Rachael was a client who had great intentions. She had a positive attitude, tremendous energy, and great personality and was well liked by everyone she met. Rachael had an amazing ability to make friends with everyone. She had this wonderful way of warming up to people so that they just naturally trusted her. By the end of a conversation, Rachael knew their life story.

Rachael had absolutely no ability to manage

her time. She was engaged in a lot of activity but she always seemed to be doing the wrong things at the wrong times. When she hired me, everything about her life was in disarray, her personal life, her relationships, her home, her professional life, and her priorities. Even her conversation shifted from one topic to another without a logical sequence.

On the physical level, she was experiencing arthritis in her leg and was holding a lot of tension in her neck and shoulders. She also told me she couldn't breathe deeply.

Rachael was also preoccupied with looking back upon her past with regret. She was consumed with anxiety over her past mistakes and couldn't see her way forward to living a life of deep satisfaction, fulfillment and success.

Rachael had a consulting business. She had some simple systems in place and was making a lot of contacts for her business but she wasn't using the systems effectively at the right times and in the right way to make them work for her.

She had a natural marketing and sales ability but she was setting goals for herself that were unachievable. She was totally overwhelmed and the distractions in her personal life were taking the focus off her business.

She wanted to be more successful but didn't know where to start. As a result, she was treading water, and going nowhere. The first thing I taught Rachael was this:

If you're always facing backward, you can't possibly move forward.

I showed Rachael how to stop, turn around and face forward. Rachael learned how to let go of her past, to turn her focus toward her goals and concentrate on what she wanted to accomplish.

I taught her how to breathe naturally and deeply by using a special technique that activates specific hormones to relieve stress. This is a technique I learned long ago when I first became a singer. Breathing helped Rachael release tension, relax and start to focus.

After a few short weeks, her arthritis disappeared, the tension in her neck and shoulders was gone and for the first time in a long while, she felt as though she had the space and permission to breathe and to be successful.

Over the course of several months working together, Rachael learned to clear her mind of the clutter. She learned to set priorities and to focus on what she really wanted for the first time in her life.

She began to make better choices because for the first time in her life, she was really thinking about the choices she was making. Rachael learned how to set reasonable goals for herself-- in her personal and professional life.

She also kept a journal to keep track of her time. This had the added benefit of helping her stay focused. It helped her eliminate those regular unproductive routines and habits that were keeping her stuck.

She cleaned up her home and gave away everything in her environment that was cluttering her life. She ended a long-term relationship that was not serving her. She started exercising regularly and began to lose the unwanted weight she had gained due to poor eating habits and stress. Her energy level increased and she felt lighter on many levels.

Rachael began to let go of her fear of success.

As a child, she felt invisible and never received validation for her thoughts. She never learned how to feel successful so she believed she didn't deserve success.

This coaching process helped Rachael to see herself differently. She began believing in herself. She started believing she deserved to be successful.

Rachael started treating her business like a business, as opposed to a hobby. She organized her checkbook and bank accounts as she learned how to respect her money. She began to learn new ways to use social marketing to improve her business results. She learned to keep track of and use her time more efficiently.

By focusing on her business in the right ways, she began to do the right things at the right times--planning, setting intentions and goals, tracking results and taking the right actions to become more successful. Implementing these strategies had the effect of improving all aspects of her personal *and* professional life.

Rachael is still improving upon all the strategies she learned in her coaching sessions with me. She is happy and optimistic about her future as she continues to grow her business.

If you're not aware, or mindful of how you spend each minute or hour of your time, then how can you possibly find the time to do more of what you want? Consciously becoming aware of how you spend your time will help you to do the right things at the right times in the right ways.

1. When you're working on something, make a commitment to stay focused until it's done. If you stay focused on what you're doing, you'll be able to accomplish more in less time.

2. If you remain aware of how you spend your time, you'll be much more efficient with it and will waste less of it.

3. If you stay present in each moment of each hour you're awake, you won't wonder where the time went because you'll know.

You will be in control of your time.

This presence of mind and awareness of what you do with your time will help you sort out which activities you should be doing at the appropriate times.

This new perspective alone will give you freedom, confidence and the perception of having more time because you'll be more aware of your time and how you're choosing to spend it. When you work this way, you'll be less likely to waste time on unproductive activities and you'll start to see immediate results.

If you take action right now and implement this Time Management Strategy into your daily routine to keep track of how you spend your time, if you make a conscious decision to DO THE RIGHT THINGS AT THE RIGHT TIMES, you will create and save more time!

Strategy # 3
Systemize and Take Control
Over Your Time

Why do you really want *more time*?

• Do you think it will make you happier?

• Will it give you a greater sense of freedom?

• Will it give you the *Feeling* that you have more control over your life?

I happen to believe it's all of the above. Your time is valuable and important to you. Don't just give it away without first considering who, or what you are giving it away to.

How you spend your Time doing anything is how you spend your Time doing everything.

Isn't it true that if we spend *more time* at a given activity, then somehow we'll be more successful at it or at least we'll feel we accomplished something?

If we spend just 5 minutes at an activity, was that a valuable use of our time? We probably don't think so because we *didn't spend much time* at it.

Life has an amusing way of rewarding us for the time it takes us to accomplish the things we do. In short, we are rewarded for the *amount* of time we spend at something.

Did you ever hear this growing up: *"How much time did you spend on your homework?"* The obvious implication was that it takes time to learn, so if you spent more time on your homework, you would learn more, master the lessons and grow up to become successful.

Do you ever hear this at work: "How long will it take you to come up with a solution?" "How much time will it take to complete the project?" Over the course of my career, I've learned something very valuable:

It's not how much time we spend on something that matters.
What really matters is
How we spend the time we have.

Yet we measure our effort and reward our results based on time.

Did you know:

•You can achieve more learning and master a technique in 15 minutes if you *really focus* on what you're doing?

•You can burn more calories in 10 minutes if you choose the right exercise?

•You can connect more deeply with those you love if you *look deeply into their eyes* than if you spend an hour with them sitting on the couch watching television?

We think something requires a lot of our time to make it worthwhile. Why?

We've been conditioned to believe this and we've been rewarded for our time.

Have you ever heard this phrase? "You have to put in your time." You were probably told at some point when you started your career that you would be expected to put in long hours because "That's what's expected of you to get ahead in this company."

Sometimes the corporate norms and culture we work in dictate how much time we spend on the job. But is it really necessary? Could we be more efficient with our time and complete what we *need* to do and have time left over for more of what we *want* to do?

The answer, of course, is yes, but we choose not to go against the established habits or system we created for ourselves or the one dictated by the culture we work within.

The problem is, this "system" doesn't work, because today we choose to do more within the time we have, and that conflicts with our modern needs to have it all--career satisfaction, family, health, wealth, happiness, freedom of choice and *more time.* In short, we end up with less of everything and wonder why we don't have a better life.

In 1992, when I was negotiating for a position to work with an Executive Education Firm based in Cambridge, Massachusetts, the partners were reluctant to agree to let me work from my home office. The concept of working from home was still relatively new. I was negotiating for a new position as the U.S. Marketing Director.

This was a new position for the company. The partners were hesitant to agree to let me work from home because *they couldn't keep track of my time.* It was clear to me that commuting to an office an hour away from my home each way would be a *waste of my time.*

I could be far more efficient working from my home office. I explained to them that it wasn't their job to keep track of my time. *What was important, were the results I achieved with my time.* My job was to market their services and sell million dollar customized executive education programs to Fortune 500 corporations with hundreds of executives.

Of course I understood the concern over their Investment, I offered to send them summaries of the contacts I was making, the companies I was visiting and the progress on my marketing efforts. They would be able to see fairly quickly if the systems I used were going to yield the results they wanted. I was confident I could deliver on my promises and my commitment.

They hired me.

I had just left my job at Harvard Business School as Assistant Director of Executive Education. I began leveraging the contacts and relationships I had made there, in this new job.

The sales cycle for these types of programs was anywhere from 6-18 months. I had to find the companies ready to invest in these programs and sell them on our customized process. It was in my best interest to make high quality, profitable sales quickly.

I immediately set up systems to make contacts with prospects and to arrange sales calls and meetings. I developed a regular reporting process and arranged meetings between the partners and clients ready to buy our customized process.

The partners became more comfortable with the new systems they had never used before. I went into the office once a week to have face-to-face meetings with the partners and gain agreement on which companies to pitch.

The new process was very effective and

successful within a very short period of time. I worked from home and traveled on their behalf, and sold millions of dollars in customized executive education programs.

I was far more productive not wasting commuting time. The systems I implemented helped me stay focused and organized to achieve the results we all wanted. It was a win-win situation and they learned to trust me with my time.

What mattered most in that position was HOW I spent my time, not *how much time* I spent on the job.

Once I had the systems in place and I had achieved success, I replicated the whole process and did it all over again, several times.

I. You can create Systems to organize any aspect of your personal or work life. Here are some examples of Effective Time Management Systems I have put in place:

Create a list system.

Write out everything you need to do and then

group the items together by name of project, similarity, geography or importance. You can even color-code projects if that helps.

Prioritize.

Prioritize your lists and organize activities every day. Decide what you really need to accomplish each day and each hour. In order to create a sense of accomplishment, check items off as you complete your projects.

Systemize your planning.

Put in time up front to plan out a project. My mom was a master organizer. When I was younger, she used to plan out all her menus for the entire year during our Christmas vacation. She would sit at the dining room table with reams of paper spread before her as she did her planning.

For example, she planned ahead of time to serve steak, French fries and green peas every third Sunday of every month. Those menus helped her know ahead of time what she was going to prepare and how much food she needed to buy every month. This helped her plan how much money she needed to budget for food. I remember piles of canned goods stacked up in the basement at home.

I have used similar strategies to systemize my planning, countless numbers of times on personal as well as professional work assignments. Although this will take time, planning is essential to getting a job done right the first time. In the long run, putting systems in place will actually save you time.

Schedule similar activities together.

Determine which tasks can be coupled with others. Read and respond to email while waiting in line or in a lobby. Run all of your errands at the same time instead of making repeat trips.

Use automated tools.

There are many automated tools available to handle email, voice mail and social media. For example, there are automated systems that can help you manage all of your social media applications so you can save time.

Schedule specific blocks of time to work on important projects each day.

I block out early morning hours for writing, marketing and meetings, etc., when my mind is clear and I have the most energy.

Organize all your calendars in one handy place.

I went from having four calendars in different places to using one. I use a mobile device that automatically syncs with my computer so I only have to enter the information once. That saves me massive amounts of time not doing double entry. I keep track of my time, my kids' time and even my husband's travel schedule. If you do this, you can determine how you regularly spend your time, so you can realistically plan out your days, weeks and months ahead.

Keep track of how you spend your Time.

Set up a time tracker, use an automated system like a mobile device, or **keep a journal** to record how you spend your time during the day. Just notice which **habitual activities** you can cut out that aren't helping you so you can make room for the things you want to do that *are* in your best interest.

Schedule client meetings and appointments on specific days.

This frees up time for the rest of the week for inspiration, play and real work.

Take note of what you accomplished at the end of the day.

Check things off your list. Reorganize and prioritize those items you still need to accomplish the next day.

Set up a regular system of pampering and rewarding yourself

Celebrate your successes when you've accomplished short and long-term goals. Make sure you match the reward to the achievement to help sustain your focus. I like to buy myself flowers for the office.

Set up a weight management and exercise system you can stick to.

Did you know that healthy eating and exercise actually save you more time? If you've been meaning to shed those extra pounds, you'll achieve twice as much every day because shedding pounds will actually give you more energy. You won't feel tired all the time, you won't have the mid-afternoon slump, you'll be far less stressed, you'll think more clearly and you'll accomplish more in less time.

Ask for help or hire professionals.

Systematically have someone else take care of activities like house cleaning, taxes and lawn care unless you absolutely love to do these things. You can't do it all. Enlist others to help you when you're in a bind. For example, I prefer to have the dry cleaners iron our table linens after a party. I find that ironing linens is too time consuming and professionals can do it far more efficiently than I can.

Time Management Case Study 1: The McKinnon Family

A good example of the importance of time management and asking for help is one that involves my youngest son. He came to me and told me he desperately wanted a new XBOX Game. I asked him if he had any money to pay for it, to which he replied, "No".

I needed to get the yard cleaned up after the heavy snowfall we had in New England this winter, so I suggested to him that if he raked and cleaned up the entire front and back yard, I would pay him for the work and he could use that money to buy the video game he wanted.

I hadn't finished my sentence when he was out the back door heading to the shed to find the rake! He cleaned up the yard all by himself in a little over two days. We went to the store together so he could buy the game.

This is a great example of how we both got what we wanted. I got an immaculate yard (which I didn't have the time to clean up) and my son got his new game. Having to work for his reward was a great way to teach him the value of *his* time.

Time Management Case Study 2: The McKinnon Family

Another example of an Efficient Personal Time

Management Tip involves my husband. He travels frequently for his job *and* he loves to cook. He and the boys cook together on weekends. It's a great family ritual and a wonderful way for the boys to become self-sufficient. They follow the recipes they want to try and prepare a variety of meals together.

What we don't eat right away we freeze and save for the rest of the week or we eat at some future date. We have another freezer in the basement where we can store the extra meals.

This saves me from having to take time to prepare and cook dinner every night, especially when we all have to be out somewhere.

It also means we have to be efficient with our grocery shopping once a week instead of making *multiple trips* to the store. I make a list of the food we need and organize the items on the list according to where the groceries are found in the aisles of the store.

This takes a little time as I write the list out; however, it reduces the amount of time at the grocery store and prevents me from roaming aimlessly looking for items.

Whatever the job-- setting up systems to take care of activities can be a lifesaver and a great time saver.

Your time is valuable. Do the quick hits first, spending time on the things you know you can accomplish easily and you want to do that give you fulfillment and enjoyment.

Then employ some of these other strategies to the longer, more difficult projects. You'll find you won't waste as much time procrastinating because you will have developed a progressive system of accomplishing your goals and you won't have as much of a desire to put things off.

II. Time Management Tactics for systemizing your day:

Here are some strategies for systemizing activities during your day so that while working on short-term goals, you're making room in your life for your long-term goals too. These techniques have worked for me and many others who need to find more time in the day or evening.

Begin your day with good habits.

Do you struggle to stay focused? Do you feel constantly starved for time, hurrying through the day while fighting countless distractions? You may have created bad habits. One way to change this is by bringing new rituals into your workday to *help create awareness.*

If you take a moment to notice what you are about to do, you remind yourself to appreciate and focus on the task, rather than rushing through it. Rituals give you space to organize your thoughts. Repeating rituals can help you create new habits and release old ones.

Plan out your day.

Map out everything you need to get done and how much time you think everything will take. Then add in a little extra time for the unexpected things that will inevitably creep into your day.

That will give you an idea of the pace in which you need to move through each project. If you know you have to accomplish a lot in a short amount of time, you'll move yourself along more quickly.

Use Efficient Email tactics.

I've put this up front because email is one of those "tasks" most of do first each day. I find that email is a blessing *and* a curse. Here are a few ways you can handle email more efficiently so that you won't be a slave to your in box:

Before your turn on your computer or pick up the phone at the start of your day, just pause. When you sit down at your desk in the morning, take a few deep breaths and **think about what you need to accomplish**. Do this exercise every time you begin a new project or assignment.

This practice will help you remain calm and centered to accomplish tasks more carefully and productively.

Don't rush to reply to your email right away. When you turn on your computer in the morning, briefly scan your email to take note of those from clients and changes to your daily schedule but unless it's urgent, don't reply. Close your email and get to work on something that helps you monetize your business or create more sales, profit or value for your company. Then after you've accomplished the important tasks, look at your email again and delete those you're not interested in to clean out the clutter. Don't reply unless it's *really* urgent. Read and reply to your email after you've completed major tasks for the day, and you've accomplished something. I wait until the end of the day to do this.

- Don't think you have to respond to all the mail you're copied on.

- If you want someone to take action on an email, write directly to him or her.

- Shorten your emails to get a quicker response.

- Clean out your inbox at the end of the day when there are fewer distractions. You'll have less email to address in the morning.

- Remove yourself or unsubscribe from email lists at least once a week. If you find you're deleting a lot of emails and not even opening them, get them off your list! This one tip will reduce the email in your inbox and save you time from looking at it, so you won't be tempted to open it

Employ Efficient Social Media tactics.

Did you know the average person spends 30 or more minutes a day on social media sites? That equals approximately 182 hours a year or 7.5 full days a year spent on social media--That's a full week out of every year! Wouldn't you rather be spending that time on vacation or doing something else you love?

- Unless you use social media for business, I don't recommend you check your face book status more than once or twice a day. Don't tweet or blog more than once or twice a day.

- Choose specific days of the week and times of the day to blog or add comments to forums or invite people to join your network. I designate blocks of time at the end of the day for social media. It's a more efficient use of my time and helps me stay focused. As a result, I get more done every day and I have a greater sense of accomplishment when I go to sleep. People also see my messages and posts in the morning, which is the peak time when others read email.

Systemize Other Daily Tasks.

- **Break up larger projects.** If you need help getting organized, break up bigger projects into smaller assignments that are more manageable. Break out each phase of a project with a start date, milestone dates, and target end date.

- **Start at the end and work backwards.** Identify your deadline date first, and then work back from that date to determine when each phase needs to be started and completed. Put larger projects up on a spreadsheet and identify specific tasks for each phase of the project.

- **Estimate how much time you think each phase of a project will take.** I move deadlines for some phases back two weeks prior to the due date, in the event unforeseen circumstances cause delays. This gives me a cushion to get things done on time or early. This step will give you an idea of how much time you'll need to do the entire project. If you're working with a team, list the names of those who are responsible for each phase and come to an agreement about deadlines.

- **Delegate** tasks to others to get the help you need.

- **Keep the status of long-term projects public.** Whether it's your family or your team at the office, if there are many projects and people involved, put everything on a white board and positioned it in a place where people gather so you can all share in the status of the projects and celebrate, as you complete your goals.

Or make the same information available

on a spreadsheet that can be shared or sent out to the team regularly as the status of the projects is updated. This keeps everyone apprised of the status without having to hold extra meetings.

- **Set deadlines and stick to them**. Some of my clients *don't set clear deadlines* to finish an activity. What happens next is that the activity often doesn't get done or it falls through the cracks as other activities take precedence. Others give themselves *too much time to get something done*. This can drag the project out and it may take forever to complete. Many people just *don't give themselves enough time* to complete a project. This only means the finish date will have to be constantly moved up as milestone dates and deadlines fail to be met.

- **Designate someone to be responsible for moving a project along.** This person keeps track of deadlines, the status of projects, what is needed and issues that arise. Whether it's you or someone you designate, this person's role is crucial to keeping everything on track.

- **Running Meetings.** Keep them short, under an hour. Invite only those who need to be there. Start on time. Have an agenda. Never serve food. Don't allow cell phones or other mobile devices in the meeting. Keep track of the time with a watch or timer. End the meeting as planned to respect other people's time.

- **Take a break and repeat.** Take 10-minute breaks between extended projects and start again. Before long, you'll have crossed enough off your list to restore yourself to a calm state of mind.

In 1979, I was hired to work for the Marketing Division as a Member of the 1980 Winter Olympic Organizing Committee. I was responsible for completing over 300 projects in three languages, on budget, within 12 months and prior to the start of the Olympic Winter Games.

From signage, tickets, maps and brochures, to Olympic Uniforms and Olympic Medals, these projects were among the most visible to the public. I used my organizational and team-building skills to complete every project successfully before the start of the 1980 Olympic Winter Games.

My reward was that I got to actually be part of and enjoy the Games, especially the famous ice hockey match between the U.S. and the USSR. Whether automated or not, whether you use tools or not, systems can help you save time. Systems can also help you take control over your personal and professional time so that you have more of it to enjoy.

You know yourself better than anyone else knows you. You know how you work. Be realistic and honest about how much time something is going to take to complete. Allow for the unexpected and set reasonable deadlines. If you keep your eye on the finish line, you'll get there more quickly.

If you take action right now and implement this Time Management Strategy and these tactics into your daily routine, TO SYSTEMIZE AND TAKE CONTROL OVER YOUR TIME, you will create and save more time!

Strategy # 4
Use Your Time and Your
Learning Style to Your Advantage

**What do you want to accomplish?
Start by establishing short-term
and long-term goals.**

When it comes to having enough time for
everything--your career, your business and
your personal life, there's a careful balance
between keeping your eye on the finish line, or
your long-term goals, and focusing on your
short-term goals.

There are a thousand things you could be
doing--managing clients, projects and cash
flow, organizing your space or desk, taking
care of the kids, working out, spending time on
hobbies, cleaning the house, volunteering.
When it comes to managing your time, you
have to look at your short-term goals *and* your
long-term goals.

Let's say you really want to take a course,
write a book, get another degree, or have
enough financial stability for retirement. You

have a huge desire to meet this goal but in the meantime, you need to make a living.

Short-term goals are those goals you need to focus on in the next 30-90 days and long-term goals are 12-18 months out. You can see it's important to pay attention to both.

If you focus only on the new long-term project you're passionate about, you're going to lose focus on your job or business and you could run into serious trouble. And if you focus only on your work, you're going to lose your enthusiasm, and feel like you're going nowhere and not really making those steps to move ahead in your personal life.

Over the course of my career, I have worked with many types of hard working individuals and clients. I have also noticed that people spend time in different ways and each has what I call a basic learning style and a "Time Profile" or predominant way in which they tend to spend their time.

While this evidence is anecdotal, and my observation, it's worth noting, because *how we do anything is how we do everything.* It's how we show up in the world. If you are aware of How you learn and how you prefer to do things, you can make adjustments when you need to.

If you are totally unaware of how you show up in the world, how you approach any task or goal, and how you learn, it's going to take you longer to get things done and it will be much harder to be flexible, and make a change when needed.

I. What's your *"Time"* Profile? How do you use your Time?

Are you an Over-Achiever?

Maybe you prefer to get things done, to do things fast. You have the energy to accomplish a great deal. This zeal is commendable, but in your haste, you may end up leaving out a few details. You're efficient and well organized. You can multi-task with ease. You're always cleaning up after yourself or others and filling your time with lots of things to do to feel needed. You probably have many "to do lists" and enjoy checking things off with ease. Accomplishing things means a lot to you. You fill up the time because you wouldn't know what to do with yourself if you had nothing to do. You like to create projects and might have several going at the same time. You spend much of your time doing things for others.

Do you Procrastinate?

Goals? What goals? You put things off. You may have every intention to get things done; however, you allow yourself to get distracted and experience the "Bright and Shiny Object Syndrome," where you allow new things to get in the way of your intended goal.

You may feel a slight resistance to finishing something or you may even believe you can't do as good a job as you set out to do. A lot of projects are left incomplete or for others to finish. Things take much longer to accomplish than anticipated. Goals keep getting pushed out and the end result is that you often fail to complete what you set out to accomplish.

One advantage to working this way is that you're not afraid to try new things. You may also be good at multi-tasking because you like to focus on more than one thing at a time. The disadvantage is that you may often miss important deadlines. This can reflect poorly on your organizational skills.

Do you prefer to be Spontaneous?

You don't intend to, but you never seem to set aside enough time to get things done. You arrive late for everything-- for meetings, appointments, and work and maybe even for your child's soccer game. You don't do this consciously. You just let time slip through your fingers and you lose track.

You require the need to be free and loose and being late gives you some sense of control over your "out-of-control world." Your desk and office, your purse, and even your wallet most likely look free and loose with papers scattered everywhere. You may be viewed as disorganized, and you fail to plan.

Spontaneous individuals have an advantage at being flexible, since you focus more in the moment, one day at a time, versus living each day on a schedule or according to plan.

The disadvantage is that you probably suffer

throughout your life, since a time management plan is not your strength so you may fail to create short- or long-term goals.

Are you a Perfectionist?

You need to get things right. You are focused, and you love getting into the details. You don't always trust others to do the job the way you would do it so, as a result, you may end up doing a project over and taking longer to get something done than originally intended. You can become engrossed in activities and can lose track of time.

You often find yourself working late to make sure everything is done just right. While this focus is admirable, you may fail to see the bigger picture and this may cause you to become confused about why you're not reaching your long-term goals and intended desires.

Missing the details, only seeing the big picture, putting things off, not showing up on time, not committing to and implementing short- and long-term goals may be the very things standing in your way of success.

Any of these characteristics may be the thing preventing you from having more freedom and more time to do what you want.

How you spend your time and how you use your time are just two ways you appear to others. It can make the difference between success and failure.

These profiles may seem a bit extreme. I acknowledge they are based on anecdotal research and you may approach life with some combination of all four. But based on my years of experience working with thousands of executives, I have observed that especially when people are under pressure or stress, they tend to revert back to a predominant characteristic when it comes to the way they spend their time.

II. What's your predominant Learning Style?

Dr. Howard Gardner, professor at Harvard University School of Education in Cambridge, Massachusetts, developed the concept of "Multiple Intelligences".

Dr. Gardner believes intelligence results from

more than one single factor, and that it can't be measured by a simple IQ test. His theory is based upon research that suggests there are multiple forms of intelligence and that we access this intelligence using our own unique learning style.

We learn best using one predominant Learning Style, which means we require *time* to process information in our own, unique way to help us experience and function in the world.

This work has had a profound impact on thinking and practice in education, especially in the United States. According to this research, there are Three Predominant Learning Styles: Visual, Auditory and Kinesthetic.

Do you know how you process information? Do you know your individual learning style?

VISUAL: Learn through seeing…These learners need to see the presenter's body language and facial expression to fully understand the content of a lesson. They tend to prefer sitting at the front of the room to avoid visual obstructions (e.g. people's heads).

They may think in pictures and learn best from visual displays including: diagrams, illustrated textbooks, overhead transparencies, videos, flipcharts and handouts.

During a lecture or classroom discussion, visual learners often prefer to take detailed notes to absorb the information. If you are a visual learner, you learn best by reading or "seeing" the concepts--diagrams, flow charts, time lines, films, flip charts, videos and demonstrations.

AUDITORY: Learn by Listening...These learners learn best through verbal lectures, discussions, talking things through and listening to what others have to say. Auditory learners interpret the underlying meanings of speech through listening to tone of voice, pitch, speed and other nuances. Written information may have little meaning until it is heard. These learners often benefit from reading text aloud and using a tape recorder. If you are an auditory learner, you learn better when you listen, or hear something told to you--hearing spoken words, participating in discussion and explaining things to others.

KINESTHETIC OR TACTILE: Learn by Doing...They need to experience learning by moving, doing, touching, or by getting personally involved. If you are a kinesthetic learner, you process information best when you're *doing* something, standing up, moving around, or working with your hands. You need to "actively" participate using your body.

What does this have to do with managing your time?

Time Management Case Study: Sandy

One of my clients was preparing for an important Financial Planning Exam. She had failed it the first time and was dragging her feet studying for the upcoming exam because the book was so tedious. When I asked her what her learning style was, she didn't know.

I explained the concept of Multiple Intelligences and Learning Styles to her and immediately she recognized *she was an auditory learner!* She always absorbed information better when she heard it.

I asked Sandy if she could access any of the study material on tape or CD. She said she could. This totally changed the way Sandy went about preparing for this exam and she even enlisted the help of her daughter to read study questions and answers to her aloud.

Within a month, Sandy had passed her exam with flying colors!

Passing this exam made a profound difference to her career. Sandy was promoted into a new assignment within her company and is moving up steadily within the organization.

Do you take advantage of your predominant learning style when you're doing your work or trying to get something done?

If you know you're a visual learner and have a deadline, use visuals to help you get it done on time. If you're an auditory learner like my client Sandy, and you need to learn new information, see if you can access it from an mp3 or CD. If it's not available that way, read into a tape recorder and play it back over and over to absorb the information more quickly. I use the voice memo feature in my mobile device for this purpose. If you're a kinesthetic learner like my husband and children, you probably need to walk around when you're trying to solve a problem.

When you break up any task or assignment into segments using your predominant learning style, it doesn't feel like work. Because you're keeping your mind interested, your mind stays focused longer so you can accomplish more in less time. This gives you more freedom, because you've now just freed up a little bit of your day to do what you want.

Understand your time profile. Find out what your unique learning style is. Use this information to your advantage. If you use this in a way that best suits your needs, you'll absorb information more quickly and more efficiently. You'll get more done in far less time.

If you take action right now and implement this Time Management Strategy, to USE YOUR TIME AND YOUR LEARNING STYLE TO YOUR ADVANTAGE, you will create and save more time in your day!

Strategy# 5
How to Find Extra Time in Your Day

How much would an extra 6 hours be worth to you?

No other skill is as important in life than to learn how to make the best use of your time. When you look back on your life will you wish you had more of anything but more time?

There are so many advantages to time management. Managing your time can help you accomplish anything. It can help you make up for lost opportunities. Time can allow you to make more money, to make a meaningful contribution to the world.

Time can allow you to create opportunities for those things that are beyond our control, but which our hearts most deeply long for; Things such as love, intimacy, spiritual connection, self-expression, happiness, peace of mind, and a brighter future for generations to come.

It doesn't matter how smart or gifted or wealthy you are. We all have the exact same amount of time in each day. If you don't learn how to make the most of your time, you will always struggle to accomplish everything in your business, your career and your personal life.

What would you give for an extra 6 hours a week for the rest of your life? What would you do with it? Would you take a vacation or build a business? What would you do with an extra 6 hours a week for your personal life? Who would you spend it with? What would you do with that time? Would you play? Love? Travel?

Of all the gifts we've been given,
Next to life itself,
Time is the most precious.

If you take a good look at how you spend your time each day, each hour and each minute, can you really say you are spending all of your time as productively as you could? Do you think you could make better use of your time to save five minutes out of every hour?

Try this time management activity:

Set aside an hour where you can really keep track of your time. Get a timer and set it to 60 minutes. A simple egg timer or stopwatch will work. Do your activity within that hour. When the timer goes off, write down how you spent the last 60 minutes.

1. Write down every detail: What did you do for the first 15 minutes, the next 15 minutes, and so on.

2. Write down what intention you set for yourself at the beginning of those 60 minutes.

3. What goals did you plan to complete in those 60 minutes?

4. What you were thinking about during that hour?

5. Record your feelings while those 60 minutes passed.

6. What did you accomplish within that hour?

7. Did you meet your goals?

8. If you fell short of your goals, what happened? Did you take a phone call? Did you get distracted by something or interrupted by someone? How much longer do you estimate it will take you to accomplish your goal?

If you accomplished exactly what you set out to do, congratulations! Did it take you the entire hour to do what you intended? Or did you finish early and move on to something else?

If you really keep track of your time during one hour of any given activity, you will find you can save yourself time. How? If you really focus and lay out the hour as instructed above, you will finish as you intended.

As you begin to use this process, you'll start to accomplish your goals early. You will find you can gain as much as 5, 10 or even 15 minutes in an hour. If you meet your goal early, set the timer and go on to the next project to complete within 60 minutes. Do it again. If you do this for 8 hours straight, how much time did you gain?

Let's say you gained 15 minutes out of every hour just by doing the short activity above. *That's 120 minutes you gained within 8 hours.* If you add that up over the course of 5 days, that's *10 hours of free time* you just saved yourself! That's an entire workday for some executives.

If you multiply 10 hours by 50 weeks (*assuming again you take 2 weeks vacation*), *that's 500 hours or approximately 21 days per year you just gained!*

What would you do with 10 extra hours a week? What would you do with 21 extra days per year?

Would you get more sleep? Would you play? Take time off? Read a book? Spend time with friends or those you love? Exercise or engage in a hobby?

Of course this is hypothetical because realistically you're going to be spending some of those 8 working hours having lunch, attending meetings, picking up the kids, doing errands, running to meet clients, etc. But I hope you get my point.

Even if it's not 15 minutes out of every hour that you save, even if it's only **5 minutes** within every hour of the 8 hours you're working, *that's 40 minutes of FREE time you get to do something you really want to do during your day.*

What would you do with 40 minutes of free time each day?

Where can you find this extra 5 minutes in an hour?

- Do you spend some of your free time each day in idle conversation because you're waiting to get on with the next task?

- Do you spend time in meetings when you could easily conduct that time on a conference call or on Skype?

- If you are the one conducting a meeting, are you setting a time limit for it?

- If you are at your desk all day working on a project, are you really spending all of your time at it, or do you find yourself drifting off, surfing the web, checking social media accounts, reading the news or getting up frequently to refill your coffee cup or get a snack?

- Do you allow yourself to be interrupted by phone calls or colleagues who want to pass something by you?

- If you travel, how do you spend the time between meetings and flights?

- When you get home at night do you spend your time watching television? Are you too exhausted to do anything but go to bed?

- In the morning, do you spend a little extra time in bed instead of getting some exercise, which you know would be good for you?

Of course everyone needs downtime. How are you spending yours?

You choose how you spend your time and what you do with it.

Each second, minute, or hour you let pass by without *meaningful intention* is time you could have spent doing more of what you want.

You either Choose to spend time on the activities you want, or you don't.

You either act or you don't.
You either achieve the results you want with your Time or you don't.

It's all up to you.

Yes, you may have customers, clients, patients and family with needs. You have projects with deadlines and bosses and co-workers who need work from you. But all those tasks and responsibilities are going to be there tomorrow and get done by someone else whether or not *you're* still around to do them.

You are not your "To Do" List.

Has it ever occurred to you that perhaps you fill up your time with tasks because it makes you feel responsible? It makes you feel needed? It makes you feel respected?

Does standing around with free time on your hands makes you feel nervous?

If nobody ever wanted anything from you, or asked you for anything ever again, how would it make you feel?

Do you derive a sense of self-respect out of controlling other people's time?

The truth is, you don't really have control over anyone or anything except yourself.

Remember, the only things you have control over are your thoughts, your words, your feelings, your responses and actions and how you choose to spend your time.

You don't control the weather, or the world economy. You don't control if someone chooses to live or die.

You don't control any one else's thoughts or feelings, what they say or *choose* to do. You don't control any one else's time.

The truth is, you really do control how you spend your time and your time alone.

It doesn't have to be a big chunk of time. Start with baby steps. Take 5 minutes out of every hour to refocus, refresh, breathe, stretch or go for a walk. That will give you a greater sense of freedom over your time.

Then try in earnest to save just 5 minutes out of every hour. As you reach this milestone, try to save 10 minutes and then 15 minutes. You'll begin to gauge how much of your time you do control and how much of your time is spent wasted.

If you're honest with your time and you look at how you really spend your time each day, you'll be able to tighten up on those areas where you're just wasting your time.

Just notice when you're procrastinating, or taking longer to do something, or allowing yourself to be interrupted. Start to develop an awareness of the time you spend doing unnecessary activities. Then switch your focus back to your goals and get something done!

If you learn to respect the time you have while you're doing something, you'll begin to free up more time for yourself so you can spend it doing the things that matter to you. If you tighten up on just some of your activities, you'll free up time for other activities that you want to do.

If you take action right now and implement this one Time Management Strategy into your daily routine, TO FIND EXTRA TIME IN YOUR DAY, you will create and save more time!

Strategy #6
Let Go of Stress and Overwhelm

What if you knew how to let go of Feeling Stressed and Overwhelmed?

Imagine how much more time would flow into your life...

The problem with being stressed is that it's so overwhelming! It interferes with your ability to make the decisions and take the steps that can get you out of this confusing cycle and take back control over your time.

When I feel stressed by having too little time, I honestly get a little crazy. I don't enjoy it. When I allow stress to overwhelm me, it can create chaos with my family, my state of mind, with communication, with my ability to focus, my memory, my ability to sleep and my overall weight and health.

After my car accident, when I learned how to use my energy and my mind to release the feelings, patterns and behaviors that led to being stressed and overwhelmed, my life

changed forever. I am truly grateful for the peace of mind I have every day now!
Are you struggling with any of these challenges? They could be some of the reasons you're feeling stressed or overwhelmed:

- You take on too much
- You have poor organizational skills
- You can't make decisions about your next right step
- You don't say "no" when you need to
- You say "yes" out of guilt
- You like to please others
- A part of you is afraid to be clear

Add any other challenges you've noticed that lead to your being stressed and overwhelmed.

This list is important because you need to recognize that the state of being "stressed" may be a result of one of the behaviors or habits that you haven't learned to let go of or clear in your life.

- In other words, if you don't say "no" when you need to, your "to do list" gets bigger and bigger.

- When you have poor organizational skills, what you need to get done takes longer and is more challenging.

- If you are a people pleaser, you put the needs of others before your own, leading to feeling overwhelmed with what you need to get done in your own life.

- If you're afraid to be clear, you may cling to being stressed and overwhelmed as a useful distraction in your life.

The worst thing about being stressed is that it prevents us from making clear decisions. When we can't make clear decisions, we don't know what to do next. Then, we stay overwhelmed and stuck in this destructive cycle and that causes us to lose time.

Living in a state of constant stress is the Greatest Waste of Time!

Time Management Case Study: Cara

My friend and client, Cara is a good example

of someone who was living in a state of constant stress and overwhelm. Cara is a successful executive in the Real Estate industry. She had a lot going on in her business and her life. Her husband had recently retired. They had sold their home and purchased a new one several hours away from her business in the city, where she had another residence. She realized she'd be commuting several hours to be with her husband on long weekends but she needed to manage her business and be close to her clients.

When we got together, her life was in a state of chaos. She didn't feel settled with all the commuting, and while attending to the details of all the moves and personal issues, she had taken her focus off her business. Then, the recent downturn in the economy hit and her business suffered even more. She had a few clients but wasn't bringing in new business.

She had become increasingly absent-minded. Her car had been towed because she forgot to put the parking sticker on her dashboard. Then the IRS contacted her because they intended to do an audit of her business. When we got together, she was in tears and everything was spiraling out of control.

Cara had been living with so much stress for such a long time, she wasn't even aware of how bad it had gotten. She wasn't aware of how she was *attracting* one personal disaster after another into her life.

During the few hours together, I helped Cara claim back her life. She learned a process to reduce her stress, regain mental clarity and shift her focus. We discussed the steps she could take to get her personal and professional life back in order.

Over the next several weeks, she worked out a better commuting schedule and started to focus on taking better care of herself. She found ways to attract new clients and get her business back on track.

She continues to grow her thriving business. What Cara needed to do was stop the behaviors, feelings and patterns that put her in a stressful state in the first place. When she cleared these, then she was able to get unstuck and free herself from stress.

It may not seem very easy to do, but I used to be there too and I've learned how to let go of what used to stress and overwhelm me. Cara is one of many of my clients who learned how to do this successfully. If you're feeling this way, then I know you can learn to do it too.

Have you been able to identify why you become overwhelmed, and more importantly, are you aware of any reasons why you may be afraid to release stress? Without identifying these areas, any progress you make won't last. If your mind finds a good reason to stay overwhelmed, you will find a way to get and stay there.

The quality and amount of free time you have to enjoy your life will improve dramatically if you feel inspired to let go of your stress and feelings of being overwhelmed.

Do you want to release your stress and feelings of being overwhelmed?

I have to admit, it took a traumatic car accident to wake me up before I realized I had to change my life and let go of my stress. People say they want to Release Stress but then they're reluctant or hesitant to let go of the behaviors and habits that lead to this state.

Our thoughts are real and carry energy.

Thoughts lead to feelings, which lead to actions, which lead to the results that show up in your life. If you don't like the results you're getting in your life, then just observe your thoughts.

When you become stressed and overwhelmed, what do you think about? I'll bet you're thinking about how you hate the situation. I bet your thoughts are anything but grateful for the situation you're in.

When you practice using your energy to think positively and feel gratitude for any situation, no matter how stressed it makes you feel, you begin to think of more things to feel good about.

This raises your energy more and and attracts even more good thoughts and feelings. This helps you begin to take more proactive and positive actions. But when you're overwhelmed and you *resist* changing, your energy is blocked and unclear, so you resist feeling good. You stay right where you are-- stuck and even more stressed.

If you look at any situation as a gift and a lesson, no matter how overwhelming, then your whole perspective will change and so will your feelings of being stressed and overwhelmed. It will cause you to stop from moving further into the feeling of stress. It will help you move out of overwhelm.

Even if you can't possibly see the gift or lesson in the situation at the time, this shift in perspective will halt the stress for a moment and that moment will give you an opportunity to shift out of that feeling. *When you've shifted out of that feeling, you will have taken back control over your time.*

Once you release the stress, you release resistance, which makes attracting better thoughts and feelings so much easier.

Releasing resistance by releasing stress means you will automatically become more aligned with the things you've been asking for and

your desires will start to show up.
Answer the following questions about your
conflicts about releasing your stress. See if any
of them resonate with you.

1. What's the "disadvantage" to releasing
   the stress in my life?

2. Am I *comfortable* with being
   overwhelmed because it's so familiar to
   me?

3. When I'm overwhelmed, does it mean I
   don't have to focus on certain issues I
   might be afraid to look at in my life?

4. What's the "advantage" to staying
   Stressed?

5. How does it "serve me" to stay stressed?

6. Is it easier to stay the way I am?

7. If I stop being stressed, will I have to take
   responsibility for more?

These are powerful questions to help you
uncover any resistance to allowing yourself to

release your stress and feelings of being overwhelmed and out of control.

Once you know your "subconscious disadvantage or advantage" to staying where you are, you become more AWARE of your reasons for your behaviors which are causing you to choose how you respond to situations and how you spend your time.

Once you really see why you're choosing to stay stressed or overwhelmed, you'll change your perspective and your energy, and you'll see better results showing up in your life. You will begin to *Triple Your Time.*

These are just some of the Advantages to managing your time by Releasing Stress:

- When you learn how to release your stress and feelings of being overwhelmed, you'll have the mental and energetic "space" to attract more time for what you want into your life.

- When you eliminate your blocks to releasing your stress and feelings of being overwhelmed, it will automatically raise your energy. Your thoughts will be in line with your desires and you'll attract more of what you want, including more time.

- You will improve your perspective and way of thinking--you will attract more success, more abundance and more *Time* to enjoy the life you created.

When you're feeling relaxed and confident because you successfully released your stress and feelings of being overwhelmed, you'll see more opportunities that match this relaxed feeling. You'll discover how to find more Time for the things you want to do. It's your choice.

Take action right now and implement this Time Management Strategy. RELEASE YOUR FEELINGS OF STRESS. Doing so will allow abundance in all forms to flow into your life including an abundance of time.

Strategy #7
Leverage Your Time

Do you know the value of your time?

Do you know how to leverage your time so you can get the most value from it?

Have you ever calculated what your time is worth?

You can use your current income or the income you'd like to make this year. Let's start with an example of $100,000 dollars gross annual income.

Divide that number by 50 weeks (assuming you take 2 weeks vacation per year). That's $2,000 dollars. Divide that by 40 hours. Assuming you work 8 hours a day and you're actually productive non-stop, which is almost impossible for most of us, that's $50 an hour.

Fifty Dollars per hour is an example of a sample hourly value for $100,000 of income per year.

This helps you see the *minimum* value your time is worth as far as your job or business goes. Now this example is not intended to make you feel good or bad about the dollar amount of your time. It's only intended to help you see that that there are probably some things you did today that are worth $50 an hour. Maybe you worked with clients, brought in new business, or added value to your company. And there were probably some things you did today that were not worth $50 an hour.

Those activities represent *lost opportunities* when it comes to the value of how you spent your time. You can't become productive with your time doing $10 an hour jobs if your time is valued at $50 an hour.

Leverage means doing more with less. In this case, it's not what you do. Rather it's how you do it. Leverage allows you to work smarter, not harder with your time. Leveraging your time means that you replace yourself, or what you spend your time on.

1. Do you do too much?
2. Do you try to do everything yourself?

3. Do you feel as though no one can do the job as well as you?
4. Do you mistrust others, and believe no one else can get the job done right or without your help?

If you answered yes to any of these questions, then you're missing opportunities to move forward and accomplish your goals.

- When you **hire someone**, or you bring someone in to help you do those little jobs, you're helping them too. That could change their life and it could make a big difference in freeing up some of your Time, to do the things you really need to accomplish.

- When you **delegate** jobs or tasks, you're leveraging your time and giving others an opportunity to learn and be mentored.

- Likewise, when you put processes and **systems** in place to handle activities, you're leveraging your time.

- When you use tools to **automate** the

things on your list, you're leveraging and getting the most value out of your time.

Doing the laundry, cleaning the house, shopping for groceries, doing yard work, picking up the kids, doing the taxes, bookkeeping, are all activities many of us have to do. However, some of these activities just keep us busy. We could learn to leverage our time with some of these tasks.

> ### *We need to stop being busy and learn to be productive with the value of our time.*

Many women executives have deep guilt and anxiety over having someone else do some of these things for them. Getting support with housekeeping and childcare will change your life. It will free up time for you to prioritize, get focused, become more productive and put yourself in balance.

After I had my car accident, my back would go into spasms whenever I started to clean my apartment. I had no choice but to hire someone

TRIPLE YOUR TIME TODAY   103

to do the cleaning for me. I soon discovered the advantages to this:

--I didn't have to do a job I didn't enjoy which also caused me physical pain.

--I could allow someone else to do it for me.

--Spending that time doing things that were productive was a better use of my time.

--I was helping to provide a job for someone else.

Even after my back pain disappeared, I continued to have someone else clean my home. It's one of the ways I reward myself. I have to admit, having a clean home gives me such a good feeling. The state of my environment is one thing that *really* matters to me. If my home or office is disorganized or dirty, I can't function as well as if that space is organized, picked up and has a fresh, clean scent.

Having accountants do our taxes is absolutely necessary! They are experts in their field. They know the tax codes and laws. I don't have time to keep up to date with all the tax changes. What I pay them to handle this job is worth every penny and it frees up my time to stay focused on my clients and my business.

When my children were much younger, my husband and I regularly hired a sitter just to give us some time together. We would use this time to have "date nights," to play tennis, have dinner, be with friends, or just reconnect and focus on each other instead of the children.

It didn't mean we loved our children any less; it just gave us an opportunity to nourish our relationship. I think that's one of the keys to being happily married for 22 years.

The next time you're about to engage in an activity or job, ask yourself these questions:

1. Is this activity worth my time?

2. Is this activity worth more or less than the value of my time?

3. Is this the best way to leverage my time?

4. Is there something else I could be doing

that would be a better use of my time?

It's important you make this a priority to change. If you're not leveraging your time, if you're not spending time on things that are equal to the value of your time, then you'll be forever wondering how to find more time.

If you take action right now and learn how to value and LEVERAGE YOUR TIME each day, you'll be able to use this Time Management Strategy to create and save more time!

Strategy #8
Reduce and Eliminate Distractions

Do you know the number one priority in business today? It's reducing and eliminating distractions and interruptions.

There are times when you simply have too much to do. You may buckle down and focus, or like many people, you may get overwhelmed, freeze up or *look* for a distraction.

Many women I know feel totally overwhelmed by all the responsibilities they have. They take on too much, try to please everyone and run out of steam while helping others. Their responsibilities spill over from work into personal time and this causes them to lose their sense of balance.

They also allow themselves to get distracted from their "to do" list. Interruptions add to the turmoil and pretty soon that to do list has taken days or weeks longer than anticipated.

Yet when I ask them if they've ever considered

not taking on so much, or giving themselves the freedom to do things without distractions, they look at me as if I have two heads. "I couldn't possibly say no," they say.

What compels us to take on more than we're physically and mentally capable of handling? Are we afraid of disappointing someone? Are we afraid someone will think less of us if we say no? Will we be embarrassed to say no? Are we striving for some ideal sense of perfection?

Sadly, I've learned from working with many clients over the years that all of this is true. We're afraid to say no because we feel we won't measure up in some way to the ideal expectations we have created for ourselves, for our self-image and for the expectations others have of us too.

We want to have it all and be all at the same time.

However, in taking on too much, we exceed our limitations, often fail to accomplish what we set out to do, and end up disappointing others and ourselves in the process. In short, we let everyone down.

There's great value in offering service to others, volunteering your time and helping out when others need a hand. I offer my services and my advice wherever I see the need and whenever I can. However, I try to remember my limitations.

Taking on more than I know I can handle in the moment doesn't serve me or anyone else. It only sets the situation up for disappointment when expectations aren't met and when I fail to deliver on my promise to others.

Wanting to be Needed Has a Price.

The cost of wanting to be needed can take its toll on us if we don't attend to our own needs first. It can create stress, and a feeling of being overwhelmed if we serve everyone else but ourselves. Underneath this need to be wanted, loved and useful, can grow feelings of resentment, anger and guilt and feelings of being less than who we want to be, who we're capable of being.

Unlike masculine power, which is the power to

create those things that can be controlled, feminine power is the power to create those things that are beyond our control, but which our hearts most deeply desire.

These things include love, intimacy, spiritual connection, self-expression, creativity, and deep sense of purpose, meaningful contribution to the world and a brighter future for future generations.

A life well balanced, requires that we use both forms of power. This requires the awakening of a creative feminine power to bring forth what our hearts long for balanced with proper use of masculine power to execute, implement and achieve the results we desire. This utilizes a more holistic approach to managing our energy and our time.

We need to balance what our hearts desire with what we're capable of implementing. That means we must make choices.

If you don't focus on your priorities and you don't make a conscious choice about what to take on, your life will become overwhelming.

You will find a great deal of liberation in learning to say no on occasion. You'll also find it greatly frees up your Time for doing some of the other things you truly want to do. Here are some simple ways you can say no and to reduce or eliminate distractions without feeling guilty, ashamed or uneasy.

I. Strategies for Personal Time Management to Avoid Distractions and Interruptions by saying No:

The next time someone asks you to do something and you know if you oblige them, you'll feel overwhelmed, count to 10 before answering right away. This will give you time to really think about whether or not you can help out in a timely manner, before responding and automatically saying "yes."

If you must say yes to a request, ask for their involvement and help. Tell this person you have other things on your list, which take priority over their request. Their request will get done faster if they seek help from someone else or do it themselves. You won't possibly be able to deliver the results they want in the time they want it without their direct support and help. They may choose to ask someone else or do it themselves. They may choose to stay involved instead of just passing it off to you. I've found this to be a great strategy with my children.

Tell them you'd like to help another time and to keep you in mind.

Just say, "No thank you. I'm not able to help out right now."

II. Strategies for Personal Time Management To Avoid Distractions and Interruptions

Shut off your cell phone, telephone and email alerts to avoid distractions when you're in an important meeting or you're trying to get something done. If it's really important they'll leave a message, email or call back.

Close your door if you have one. If you only do this on occasion, most people will respect your need for privacy. If you don't have a door, hang a little sign asking not to be interrupted for 30 minutes. If someone interrupts you when you're working on an important project, ask him or her to hold the thought and get back to you later when you can focus on them.

If you're giving yourself a few minutes to take a break, do something *you want to do*. This is time you designated for yourself. Go for a walk, take a power nap, do a bit of stretching, do a 10-minute meditation. Find a place where you won't be disturbed or interrupted. Don't work on replying to emails, finishing memos or chatting with co-workers.

Time Management Case Study: Karen

Karen is a successful faculty member at a prestigious university. She has a full course load. She is also married with children and she primarily is the one who manages her home and family life.

Over the past few years, the stress of her job has taken its toll on her health. As a result, she developed a serious thyroid condition. She came to me for help in learning how to manage her boundaries and for help in managing her health and her stress.

She told me she was having difficulty finding time to focus her mind, meditate and relax. Every time she tried to find a moment alone, her family thought she was just resting and still available to them. They would constantly interrupt her. Clearly, her family wasn't respecting the time she'd set aside for herself because Karen hadn't told them she needed that time to be alone to relax and unwind.

I advised Karen to find a quiet place in the house where she could relax undisturbed.

I also suggested to Karen that she set some ground rules with her family and tell them when she needed some personal time at home.

This practice has helped Karen avoid a lot of misunderstanding and has given her the freedom to find some time for herself.

If you don't respect your own time, no one else will.

I always let people know when I can't be disturbed. I tell them I'll be unavailable for an hour. Until that time, if my office door is closed, it means unless it's an emergency, I don't want to be disturbed. They honor and respect my time because I set the rules and the limits for my time. During that time, I don't answer my telephone or cell phone. I eliminate distractions so that I can focus on what I need to accomplish.

If you respect your time and clearly communicate your wishes to others, they will learn to respect your time as well.

Some people use social media as a distraction from doing what they need to do. They spend too much time on face book or twitter and then rationalize it as networking. Then they wonder where the time went.

1. **Limit your time on Social Media sites** to certain times of the day or certain days of the week. Block out time to devote to Social Media as a planned activity that you put on your calendar.

2. **Don't take phone calls**: If you have a project that must get done, let your calls go into voicemail to give you control over when to return them.

3. **Do some quick hits**: Spend 15-20 minutes of your day doing some of the fastest things on your list--a quick email response, the 2- minute phone call. Use a timer or watch to keep your mind focused.

4. **Turn off Distractions:** When you need to focus on the tougher things without interruption, spend 30 minutes with your phone, radio, email alerts and notification sounds turned off. If you absolutely cannot work without background noise, then use headphones so you can tune out extraneous noise. You can also set your email to only check every 30 or 60 minutes rather than every 2 minutes. This will help you resist the temptation to open that email that just arrived!

The next time you are stressed out by how much you need to accomplish and you really need to MINIMIZE INTERRUPTIONS AND DISTRACTIONS, use this Time Management Strategy and these tactics to help you create and save more time!

Strategy #9
Save Time While You Sleep

How can you *create* more time in your day *while* you're sleeping at night?

We often view the processes around innovation and creativity as mystifying or magical. In reality, the capacity to think more creatively is natural. We were all born with the capacity to be highly intuitive and creative.

The problem is, by the time most of us reach the age of five, we start school, and over time, all that creativity is taught out of us. We're taught to follow rigid rules and ways of thinking that discount our intuition and suppress our creativity. And if we are a creative or original thinker, we're considered "different," and out of place. We just don't fit in.

Luckily, I see this changing in some school systems today. Despite much progress in this area, however, lack of innovation and creative thinking remain key issues that stall productivity in organizations.

Many companies still don't know how to implemented innovation in the work environment in a systematic way.

Despite what you may believe, creativity is something that can be systematically, enhanced and improved upon dramatically through practice.

Using sleep as a time management strategy to add more time to your day may seem odd to you. You're probably wondering, "How can I possibly save time while I sleep?

Next to breathing, sleep is our most fundamental need. It's also the first thing we're willing to give up in an effort to get more done. The fact is, even small amounts of sleep deprivation make us vastly less efficient. Getting 7-8 hours of sleep should be one of your highest priorities.

By understanding better how our brain works, and what environment serves creative thinking best, we can create a whole new path to thinking outside the box.

The following technique is one I learned many

years ago as a creativity, or innovation management consultant. It involves using your subconscious mind to solve problems.

As a consultant helping companies develop new ideas for products and brands, we had at our disposal many useful tools for helping teams generate ideas. It was our job to help executives and managers develop their own creative skills to help their companies innovate and bring new products to market.

We worked with companies like PepsiCo, General Mills, Kraft Foods, Dr. Scholl's and Clorox. Many innovative and successful new products came out of those idea-generating sessions. We took our clients through a series of processes to do that.

I'm not going to cover idea-generating processes here. If you're interested, you can contact me to discuss how I can help you or your company in this area through my coaching process.

I will share one technique though that we used successfully during the creative process--using sleep to generate new ideas and to solve nagging issues and problems.

When I first learned this time management technique, I didn't know all the brain science behind it. I just started using the technique and it worked every time. Now I use this time management tool instinctively but with intention and it yields amazing results for me.

Over the last 20 years, scientists have uncovered some truly remarkable information about how the human brain works and processes information. I'm not a scientist, but I can share with you a little about what I've learned about how the human brain helps us solve problems while we sleep and how that can actually help you not only save time, it can help you Triple your Time.

When you're awake during the day, your mind is loaded with thoughts. You have on average about 20,000 thoughts a day. That's a lot of thinking. Unfortunately, approximately 70%-80% of those thoughts are negative. Which means you spend a lot of time thinking unproductively. It's the *negative thinking* that actually gets in the way of achieving the results you want.

Your negative thoughts stop you from accomplishing what you want to do because negative thoughts create doubt and fear and that creates hesitation, immobility and inaction. If you're hesitant about the direction of your goal, then you're not achieving it. That means it will take you longer to get there. It will take more time.

So let's say you're working on an issue or problem. You've been working on it for some time. You just can't find the solution. It's taking you longer than you anticipated and now you're starting to feel the pressure. You have a deadline looming and you just can't seem to find the answer. You feel like you're just wasting your time and there's no solution in sight.

Did you know that negative thoughts don't have quite the same effect on the mind when you go to sleep with a positive intention?

During the day, your ego, your conscious mind and your sub-conscious mind all play a role in determining your habits, your actions and the results you get. When you sleep, your mind goes into a restful state but your mind doesn't stop thinking.

This is the amazing part about the human brain: when you sleep, the daily filters and negative influences are not there to disturb you. You're not consciously aware of them so it frees up a little bit of your mind to think about something else.

If you go to sleep worrying about something, the result you get might be insomnia, exhaustion, nightmares and a host of other physical symptoms resulting from lack of proper rest and sleep.

On the other hand, if you go to sleep with the intention of *solving a problem or coming up with a workable solution to a problem*, your mind will find a way to deliver a solution to you.

Your Mind Never Sleeps.

Your mind is a filter for the experiences you have in your daily life. It's like a tape recorder. It records the information you give it. If you feed it negative thoughts, that's exactly what your mind plays back to you. If you put positive thoughts into your mind, it will generate more positive thoughts. This is the way it works, every time, unless you direct your mind to do something different.

Remember, you control of your thoughts. So if you go to sleep with the positive intention of solving a problem or coming up with a workable solution to the problem, your mind will find a way to deliver a solution to you.

That's because you've given your mind something productive to do during the night, so it spends that time working to deliver what you want.

It's really ingenious. Now, the answer you get may not be the answer you were expecting, and it may not show up right away. That's the beauty of this system. The solutions our mind delivers to us are far more creative than we can *imagine*.

Most people don't realize that they have an incredible problem-solving machine in their heads and because they don't know that, they fail to take full advantage of it and use it when they need it most. Then, when they do get a solution to their problem and it pops into their head, they miss it, or dismiss it or they don't see it because they're not looking for it. And then it's gone forever...

THE PROCESS OF SAVING TIME WHILE YOU SLEEP

Before you go to sleep, gather a pen and piece of paper or notebook. This is what you are going to call your Idea Journal.

Put this Journal by your bedside.

Now, when you lay your head on the pillow to go to sleep, instead of thinking about all the ways your day went wrong, and the things you're worrying about, begin to create a new way of thinking…

Think about those things that went right during the day. Think about all the things you did accomplish.

Bring to mind all the success you had during the day, no matter how large or small. Notice how thinking about your success makes you feel in your body. Does it make you feel a little lighter? Is some of the tension going away?

Focus on your breath and allow your body to relax as you consciously bring to mind some of the things you're grateful for.

Say to yourself what you're grateful for:
"I'm grateful for my family."
"I'm grateful for my spouse."
"I'm grateful I have a job."
"I'm grateful that I have a place to live."
"I'm grateful that I can pay my bills."
"I'm grateful for my pet."
"I'm grateful I have so many interesting things
  to do with my time."
"I'm grateful to be alive."

Say a prayer of thankfulness to your God if it makes you feel good.

You want to put your mind into a state of receptive appreciation and *gratitude* and go to sleep thinking that way. You don't want to fall asleep worrying about your problems.

Now, let the issue you'd like to solve come to mind only in the following way. Say to yourself:

"I have the intention of allowing my mind to come up with a workable solution to xyz...(the issue you're working on.)"

Clearly State to yourself what the issue is. Then let go of the thought or issue…

Instead, go back to thinking about other things you're grateful for and focus on your breath. Allow yourself to drift off into sleep as you focus on your breath and you focus on relaxing each part of your body.

When you wake in the morning, see if you can remember any dreams you had. Jot them down, even if they seem strange or unrelated to your issue or problem.

Do any ideas pop into your head related to your issue? If so, write them down in your Idea Journal or notebook.

Also jot down any ideas that come to mind even if they seem unrelated to your issue. These ideas may be links to a solution you're not aware of yet. If you don't get any ideas right away, look for them during the day. Notice if you get any solutions as you continue to work on the issue.

This next step is important — be careful not to judge the solutions or ideas that come to you.

This is a creative process and you need to foster a receptive, welcoming environment for all your ideas, no matter how silly or unworkable they may seem at present. During this process, you're building a bridge with your ideas to the solution.

Allow yourself to build the bridge.

If you don't get a solution right away, repeat the process again each night until you train your mind to work for you. This process will provide a solution for you. You just have to be aware of your thoughts. Be patient and allow the solution to come to you.

Remember, it may come in an unorthodox way. For example, you might notice an article in the news that leads you to the solution; someone may say something in conversation or send you an email that creates another idea that leads to a new solution; you may notice a billboard; hear something in a meeting; or lyrics to music may provide the stimulus to create the solution.

Seemingly disconnected things and "Coincidences" will lead you to the solution and you need to be always mindful that any of these paths can get you there.

As ideas pop into your head, capture them. Write them down. Notice Coincidences.

Because I am an auditory learner, I use the voice memo feature on my cell phone to capture new ideas when I'm away from my computer. Then, when I have the opportunity, I log them into my journal or on my computer.

With this process, some tougher issues may still take weeks or months to solve. Others may only take days or even hours to solve. I had an issue that took me several years to solve but that's because I didn't pay attention to the coincidences and the connections occurring in my life.

Once you implement this system, it will be your connection to an untapped resource you've had all along but didn't know how to use properly.

This time management technique saves you time.

 It gives you time to work on the issues you can solve and it puts your mind to work to solve the issues that are not as easily within your reach.

Instead of wasting time during the day focusing on the things that are keeping you stuck, you get to work on the things that can move you forward and this has the effect of giving you more time because you reach your goal much more quickly.

If you take action right now and incorporate this Time Management Strategy into your daily routine to USE SLEEP TO SAVE TIME, you will be able to tune into your highest creative power and that will help you create and save more time!

Strategy #10
Create New Rituals to Triple Your Time Each Day

Have you unconsciously slipped into repeating the same habits and routines you've been trying to change?

Boredom creates apathy. If I do the same routines over and over, frankly, I get bored and I find myself slipping into old habits. To avoid this type of slump, I add something new to spice up my routines. I add new *rituals* to keep my routines fresh and to keep my brain interested.

Below are some of my personal rituals. If you choose to adopt just one of these during your day, you'll find you've created the space to do a little more of what you love.

Time isn't linear. But we were taught to believe it is. We were taught to live in a way where we function along this linear time line. In reality, time has no limit, no beginning and no end. Time is just a perception that expands when you focus on it. And even though time doesn't stop, when you're in the space of your own awareness for even a moment, *you will feel as though time has slowed down perhaps ever so briefly. That's when you can use time to your advantage.*

1. **When you wake each morning, before you get out of bed, decide what your primary intention is for the day.**

It may be to start a new project or complete one. It may be to get out of bed right away so you can work out or have a good breakfast. It might be to become more aware of how you spend and use your time. It may be to pay more attention to your own needs.

2. **Begin your day with good nutrition.**

You probably know the importance of getting a good breakfast, yet many people don't take the time to eat before they start their day. Is this you? Do you rush out of the house and grab a cup of coffee only to be starving and depleted by 10 a.m.? Having a good breakfast will keep your energy going so you can accomplish more during your day:

Start the day with a glass of water followed by a good source of protein. I generally eat low carbohydrate vanilla yogurt with fresh fruit, a scoop of protein powder and some form of grain or nut--like oats and almonds or walnuts.

I mix it all together because I enjoy the textures. During the winter, I sometimes mix this yogurt into plain oatmeal and add dried cherries or blueberries. During the summer, I make a milk shake out of it.

I like the ritual of having a cup of coffee. I usually have one cup in the morning but it's naturally decaffeinated and I don't need it.

This process makes a quick, delicious breakfast that keeps me full until almost noon, so that I'm not even tempted to snack in the morning. I try to listen to my body. If I do get hungry, I eat an early lunch or I have another glass of water if I can't take a lunch break yet.

3. **Eat at the right times.**

Some interesting current scientific research suggests that there is a correlation between when we eat and how our body and brain function together. There may be an optimal time of the day to eat for minimal weight gain. The research suggests that if we eat when we are supposed to be awake, versus when we are supposed to be asleep, our body's internal clock works to keep our metabolism functioning properly.

After 5:30 p.m., lipid digestion and absorption start to slow down. Eating a big meal after this may disrupt our internal clock. If you always have your biggest meal at night and you snack after that up until bedtime, it may be the reason why it's hard for you to get to sleep *and* to lose weight.

4. **Do occasional one-minute workouts**.

Research shows that kids do better in school when they get a little exercise beforehand. Why not adults too? If you have the time to work out, do so. If you don't have the opportunity to start your day with a long workout or your energy is dragging in the middle of the day, try this one-minute workout:

Stand up with your feet flat on the floor and your hands by your side. Now raise your feet up slightly so that you're resting on the balls of your feet. Gently bounce up and down on the balls of your feet for the count of 100, for a minute or so as if you're jumping rope. You can rotate your hands as if you're holding the rope and bounce with every rotation of your hands. This will get your circulation going. You can do this mini-exercise any time you need to re-charge or re-focus.

5. **Give yourself 5 minutes each hour to do something you choose to do.**

Go for a short walk, take a power nap, listen to some music, read a paragraph in a book. Do something that gives you pleasure or joy. Take care of yourself each day even if it's only for 5 minutes each hour.

6. **Let go of things that take up your time but serve no purpose.**

Let go of the "things" you do to keep "busy" because you're not sure what to do next or you want to "Feel" useful. Just stop and think, what's my most important goal for the day? Keep focusing on completing your goal. This will keep your mind on track.

7.   **Be by yourself without distractions**.

Turn off the television, radio, tune out the external distractions and just be with yourself, focusing on your breath, gently breathing in and out, with your eyes closed. Give yourself a chance to tune into your body. Breathe into that part of your body that's tight or stiff and relax. As you breathe, imagine breathing light into that part of your body that's in pain or under stress. As you breathe out, let go of the pain or stress with each exhale. Allow yourself to relax your body and your mind.

8.   **Use Visualization or Meditation to Relieve Stress and Save Time.**

Medical research has proven that using some form of visualization or meditation actually helps reduce stress, lowers the heart rate, lowers toxic levels of adrenalin and helps to increase focus. Stress is one of the main causes of weight gain, memory loss, heart disease, stroke and heart attack, immune disorders and early death.

Every day, countless news stories reveal the new benefits of meditation. Meditation has been proven to extend your life, create more happiness, increase inner peace, lower stress levels, increase mental clarity and resolve long-standing emotional problems, including fear, anxiety, depression, anger, and substance abuse.

Most people don't have the time (or patience) to invest the years of practice required to master the art of meditation. One of my purposes in being a coach is to teach and make available to people just like you the very best and most effective ways to:

- Dramatically improve your mental, emotional, and spiritual health.
- Help you create real happiness in your life, regardless of your past or present circumstances.

- Improve your creativity, intelligence, and mental functioning.
- Significantly improve your overall sense of wellbeing and inner peace.
- Help you create your own success in the world, along with the personal satisfaction and sense of fulfillment that comes with being successful.

Anytime you use a process to calm and focus your mind, you're meditating, whether or not you realize it. This includes, exercising, going for a walk, gardening or engaging in some hobby.

My mom used to iron the laundry as a form of meditation. It gave her a chance to be alone with her thoughts. It relaxed her. Choose some activity that accomplishes this end result-- quiet time to empty your mind.

In the Appendix, you'll find a simple, quick, and effective Guided Meditation, or Energy Exercise to help you release stress. This process has many benefits:

1. It calms your mind;

2. Helps you refocus during the day;

3. Helps reduce stress, which improves your productivity and creativity;

4. This process saves you time.

The Guided Meditation takes about 8 minutes. You can make it as long or short as you like and you can use it as often as you like, any time of the day when you need a moment to refocus and regain your balance. You just need to be in a place where you can quiet your mind and where you can put all your attention on the process. You shouldn't be engaged in doing anything else while using this process. Give this your full attention to get the most out of it.

Turn to the **Appendix** to access the Bonus *Guided Meditation to Release Stress.*

If you prefer the audio version of this Guided Meditation, you can find it, as well as other products to help you create and save time, in my *website store* at: http://www.kathryn-mckinnon.com/products-page/

Sincere thanks for taking some of your precious time to read this book.

Do something good for yourself today. Create new intentions and resolve to use the TIME MANAGEMENT STRATEGIES, TOOLS and TECHNIQUES in this book. Work them into your daily routine to create new, productive habits.

If you do, you'll find these strategies will help you create and save more time. They'll help you Triple Your Time Today!

Much Success,
Kathryn McKinnon

Appendix:
Guided Meditation to Relieve Stress
By Kathryn McKinnon

I am going to guide you through a meditation to help you shift the feelings of stress in your body so that you can take control over your time. Keep using this technique and notice how things begin to shift for you. Then whenever a new stress appears, use this technique to let it go. Resolve not to take stress into your body.

On a scale of 1-10, where 1 feels great and 10 feels highly stressed, how do you feel right now?

If you feel very stressed, you might feel like a number 9.

If you're feeling pretty relaxed, you may be at a number 2. Just decide where you are on this scale right now.

Now sit down, help your body get comfortable, and close your eyes.

Take a few deep breaths through your nose

and breathe deeply into your belly...Breathe in, hold it....and release your breath through your mouth. Allow your awareness to come to the center of your head so that you're fully present.

Collect up all your thoughts from yesterday, today, and tomorrow and focus your attention so that you're right here, right now, in this moment.

As you bring your awareness here to the center of your head, take a few deep breaths.

Don't worry if your mind starts to wander, just bring your awareness back to your breath as you collect your thoughts up to *rest* in the center of your head.

Now, as you take a deep breath, bring your thoughts to a time or situation when you were totally at ease, totally relaxed and happy, totally free from stress and felt as if time was on your side. It could be a time when you felt loved, when you experienced some major accomplishment, when you felt secure, when you were doing something you loved, or it could be a time when you just felt comfortable and free from worry or pressure. How did your body feel in that situation?

As you think about this comfortable, happy time or situation, allow your awareness to feel that comfort, relaxation, or happiness in your body.

Where do you feel that comfortable feeling in your body?

Visualize that place in your body now. It might be in your head, your belly, your heart or somewhere else. Imagine that place in your body that knows what comfort, peacefulness, free time for yourself, and freedom from stress feel like for you.

If you can't locate the feeling in your body, then imagine what the feeling in your body *would be like* if you had the peace, calm, TIME and freedom from stress you are looking for.

This peacefulness might take the form of doing better at work, being with someone you love, feeling as though every day flows easily and smoothly, having no pressure, having balance in your life, having an abundance of wealth, being healthy or happy.

It might take the form of people accepting you the way you are, it might be freedom from stress or craziness, the freedom of having enough time to get things done. Or do what you want.

Whatever it is, allow your awareness to go to that place in your body that knows, or can imagine that calm state, that confidence and peacefulness.

Now with every breath you take, allow that feeling of calm and peacefulness to start to grow. Allow it to expand. Allow this feeling or vibration to move through every cell of your body. Allow the feeling of freedom that comes with it to move through every cell in your body, expanding and growing.

Some people see this as a color moving through their body. Some people experience it as a warm feeling in their heart, or as a deep calm coming over them.

Other people notice it feels like a sensation, tingle or aliveness.

No matter how you experience it, allow the feeling to grow and expand and to be absorbed by your body so that every cell gets to know what true calm and peacefulness feel like.

Now allow that feeling and that vibration to fill your body. See it filling up the space around your body too so that you're glowing with this energy of peacefulness and calm. See it all around you as if you are IN a gigantic bubble and this energy fills that bubble too.

This energy can have a feeling, a color, a vibration, a tingle, an aliveness or sensation. Some people feel chills up their spine. No matter what it is for you, allow that sensation to be experienced by your body and the space around you.

Now allow your awareness to go to the space about 12 inches above the top of your head.

Imagine a golden beam of light like a spotlight coming from the space above your head and shining onto the top of your head.

Imagine this beam of light entering your head and filling your entire head with its golden

glow and warmth.
Feel this light move down through your head,
into your throat,
to your neck,
and shoulders,
down your back,
down your arms and hands,
and move down into your heart.
Feel it pulsate in your heart and through your
body as your heart beats and with every breath
you take.

Continue to feel this pulsating warm light in
your heart, as this light moves down your
back,
into your belly,
through your hips,
into your legs, knees and into your feet.

Now as you continue to feel this light, this
glowing energy, imagine that with every
breath you take, more and more of this light
enters your body so that you feel it more and
more.

Now imagine that at the bottom of your spine,
connected to your tailbone, you have a magic
slide that reaches way down and connects to

the earth, kind of like a water slide, connecting your tailbone to the earth.
In this moment, if there is something bothering or upsetting you, say to yourself:

"I acknowledge I'm experiencing something that is causing me pressure, stress or discomfort. I choose to accept myself anyway, just as I AM. "

Now take whatever is bothering you and push it down that slide into the earth. Just let it go right now. Any stress or pressure, any pain in your body, any bad or hurt feelings, any anger, guilt, grudges, any negative emotions that are not helping you or serving you. Take a moment to let it all go down the slide.

If there is a lot of stress piled up, waiting to be pushed down, just take your time to let it go…

Take a deep breath.

Now you have room in your body for a better form of energy, for better thoughts and better feelings.

Imagine that this energy, this light, as it

continues to comes into your body through the top of your head, takes the form of peacefulness, comfort, happiness and a feeling of more time to do what you want. This light washes away any remaining stress in your body.

It lifts the weight off your shoulders.

This light comes in as a feeling of deep calm raining down upon you and washing over you like a warm shower.

It rains down on you like a deep sense of freedom coming over you. It is the feeling of being safe and totally loved and accepted, in control of your time without any pressure.

It might look or feel or sound like you being *exactly who you want to be* -- right now.

This energy and peacefulness become so plentiful that you laugh and play and smile and you are *happy* being just who you are and what you want Right Now.

This peacefulness can be so plentiful that it keeps finding you wherever you go because you are in this energy.

Now imagine that you can increase this feeling even higher to the degree you want.

Go ahead and Turn up that feeling now and allow it to increase. Feel how good it feels to have all of your needs met and to be supported in every way, to be able to have this peacefulness, this time, flowing in and through you like a river and to be able to have your body recognize it and be happy in the feeling.

Go ahead and continue to feel this calm and peacefulness until you get to that place that feels safe, feels like you're home!

That place that feels like--This is what comfort feels like! This is what peace of mind feels like. This is what a stress-free life feels like. This is what having the time to do more of what I want feels like!

Allow your body to feel it, allow yourself to feel it, allow yourself to smile in it and be happy in this moment.

Now... put your *intention* on being at peace and

on being in control of your time.
Say to yourself, I AM calm,
I AM peace,
I AM Serenity,
I AM focused,
I AM intelligent and I AM doing my very best.
I AM creative,
I AM compassionate and loving,
I AM success,
I AM happy,
I AM spending my time the way I want right
now, I AM all I am capable of and all I desire to
be.

Being me is good enough.

I call forth to me all those experiences, people,
ideas and inspirations that match this vibration
and feeling.

Peace to the body, Peace to the mind, Peace to
the spirit…

End of Meditation

Now take a moment and let this connection settle into your body. As this energy settles into your body, ask yourself:

"What form will this energy will take in my life today? How can I use this vibration for my highest good in the rest of my day and night? I *wonder* how this energy will move out into all my experiences?"

Choose to set an intention for each moment-- a conscious way to live your life. Choose your thoughts carefully and always reach for a better feeling thought when you start to feel stress, or under pressure because you feel you don't have enough time.

Choose your words carefully--you can never take them back. Choose your actions carefully and live with positive intentions for your highest good and for the good of others.

Allow this to be the energy you choose to live your life from. Have fun! Enjoy your life, and enjoy the abundance of the universe and allow this abundance in all forms to flow through you more and more.

This Meditation has helped many of my clients relieve their stress and gain clarity and perspective. Many have reported that their intuition and awareness have improved along with their ability to retain information and to improve their focus.

As a result, many have improved their self-confidence and self-esteem. They changed self-defeating habits and are now able to use their time more efficiently so that they have *more time to enjoy doing what they want!*

Resolve to use this TIME MANAGEMENT TOOL starting today. Work this Meditation into your daily routine to release your stress, to increase your concentration, to improve your productivity and creativity, develop a more positive perspective and to help you refocus on your goals and objectives.

Ultimately, this Time Management Activity will **help you create and save more time. It will help you Triple Your Time Today**!

About the Author

Kathryn McKinnon
Time Management
Expert, Founder
McKinnon & Company

Successful women executives, entrepreneurs and professionals who have everything but more time to enjoy their lives, are singing the praises of Life Coach Kathryn McKinnon.

Kathryn is a time management expert, the Founder of McKinnon & Company, Executive Development and Coaching for Success, and Author of *Triple Your Time Today! 10 Proven Time Management Strategies to Create & Save More Time*

Jordan Rich from Boston's WBZ Radio says: *"Kathryn is terrific and extremely perceptive. She guides you through a learning process that allows you to gain insight into what's going on in your life."*

This former Harvard Business School

Executive turned Coach in 1992, discovered her gift for organizing and managing time when at the age of 24, she successfully managed the development and delivery of over 300 projects in 3 languages within 12 months and under budget as a Member of the Lake Placid Olympic Organizing Committee.

She went on to hone her 32 years of business expertise working with Fortune 500 firms and entrepreneurial companies as a corporate Advertising Manager, Product Manager, Marketing Director, Business School Administrator and Consultant. Kathryn received an **MBA from Harvard Business School**. She also taught the popular **Career Management Seminar** at The Harvard Business School for 6 years.

She is the founder of two businesses, has been happily married to the same wonderful man for over 20 years, is mother of two energetic teenagers, is a volunteer, Reiki Master, Radio Show Host and professional singer. For 20 years as a coach, Kathryn has dedicated her professional life to helping her clients quickly achieve greater success and order out of chaos with their life, career and their time. Here's what people have to say about Kathryn:

*"I came to Kathryn when I was anxious about assuming new work responsibilities and needed to build confidence, strengthen my voice and polish some personal skills. Our sessions were **tailor made** for me and helped me to identify, evaluate and understand what I call my "stumbling blocks." Kathryn's intuition, guidance and spiritual mentoring changed me, changed my life. Working with Kathryn, I learned more about myself in eight sessions than I ever thought possible. She helped me move forward through every step of the process and gently guided me to the place I want to be."* **Amy Dittrich**

"Your process made such a difference for me. It really helped me solve some of my biggest issues and I'm in a really good place now, thanks to you. You moved me here. The strategies and tools you gave me, and the way you supported me really helped. You challenged me and brought me to this place. I might have discovered this on my own, but you knew where I needed to go to bring me to different realizations and challenges. I still use the tools you gave me every day." **Cheryl Burns, Financial Investment Management**

"It's been a long time since I felt a lot of chaos in my life…it was you who helped me to the other side. Thank you." **Karen Dempsey Carney, Owner, Alliance Relocation/Alliance Home Loan**

"This is the longest stretch of time where I haven't felt stressed about my life. You've helped me with that. As issues have come up, you've given me guidance and helped me find answers to reasons why things are happening." **Cheryl Byrne, Communications, Issues Management Consultant**

"Kathryn McKinnon is a hidden jewel and when you find her, you know she has appeared at the right time in your life. I needed help healing recurring aches from stress and arthritis. In a few short weeks, after working with Kathryn, those issues disappeared. It is my distinct pleasure to recommend Kathryn, for her coaching for life and business. I have seldom seen anyone who cares so much about helping people to succeed and gives so much from the heart. Choosing Kathryn has given me unique ways and perspectives to learn new time management strategies and to be successful in my life and my career." **Roberta Chadis, UnFranchise Owner/ Shop Consultant** at **Shop.Com/ Market America**

Today, through her e-products, seminars, speaking engagements, private, customized coaching, radio show and her book, the strategies and tactics Kathryn shares will help you create and save the Time to do more of what you want and end each day with a sense of freedom and accomplishment.

Kathryn can help you develop the inner tools and strategies to stay organized, focused, and moving forward in your life. She will help you develop a frame of mind--a way of thinking, to help you successfully keep things on track, free up your time and reach your goals without becoming overwhelmed or giving up the things you love to do.

Kathryn is an expert at managing her own time with ease and joy. She can help you do the same. You'll learn the exact strategies, tactics, tools and action steps she uses to manage, save and create time to live a balanced, happy and fulfilled life.

Talk to Kathryn now and you'll understand the root cause of your issues and exactly what you need to do to reach your goals. If you're committed to moving forward, working with

Kathryn can give you unique ways and perspectives to achieve more success with your life, your career and your time. She can't wait to show you how.

Visit **www.Kathryn-McKinnon.com** to learn more.

Services offered:
Personal, Customized One-on-One Coaching and Mentoring,
Corporate Coaching
Group Coaching,
E-Based products, Courses, Books
Speaking,
Seminars and Training

Contact Kathryn McKinnon:
Founder and CEO
McKinnon & Company
Executive Development &
Coaching for Success
21 Robert Rd. Marblehead, MA 01945
1-781-631-2193 (EST)
McKinnon_Company@comcast.net

Join her Networks and continue to receive information about new Time Management

Strategies, Tips, Techniques and Case Studies featured on her website, blog, twitter, linkedin and facebook fan page posts:

http://www.Kathryn-McKinnon.com
http://www.Kathryn-McKinnon.com/blog
http://twitter.com/KathrynMcKinnon
http://www.linkedin.com/in/KathrynMcKinnon
http://www.facebook.com/pages/Kathryn McKinnonCoaching

Visit **http://www.Kathryn-McKinnon.com** to sign up for Kathryn's FREE Ezine where she shares more of her secret Time-Saving Strategies and Tips!

66207228R00087

Made in the USA
Columbia, SC
16 July 2019